YOUR KNOWLEDGE HAS VALUE

Mirja Quix

Bart Simpson in Place of the Bard

The depiction of Popular Culture in Anne Washburn's Mr. Burns, A Post-Electric Play

GRIN Publishing

Bibliographic information published by the German National Library:

The German National Library lists this publication in the National Bibliography; detailed bibliographic data are available on the Internet at http://dnb.dnb.de .

Imprint:

Copyright © 2014 GRIN Verlag, Open Publishing GmbH
Print and binding: Books on Demand GmbH, Norderstedt Germany
ISBN: 978-3-668-01005-5

This book at GRIN:

http://www.grin.com/en/e-book/302770/bart-simpson-in-place-of-the-bard

GRIN - Your knowledge has value

Since its foundation in 1998, GRIN has specialized in publishing academic texts by students, college teachers and other academics as e-book and printed book. The website www.grin.com is an ideal platform for presenting term papers, final papers, scientific essays, dissertations and specialist books.

Visit us on the internet:

http://www.grin.com/

http://www.facebook.com/grincom

http://www.twitter.com/grin_com

Table of Content

Introduction

"...and thank you most of all for nuclear power, which has yet to cause a single proven fatality. At least in this country. Amen."

It is this prayer that Homer Simpson, the head of the well-known yellow television family, states one episode while breaking bread at the supper table (comp. Broderick 2004: 252).

A main objective of *The Simpsons* series seems to be to take every day issues and world events as a part of its stories and to deal with them in a satirical way. While it also concerns itself with apparently banal issues like popular movies or bands, war, politics or nuclear power do not make an exception in the series' content. Mick Broderick points out, that

> *"while many episodes ostensibly do not touch on nuclear themes, the ever- present influence and immanence of the atomic age pervades* The Simpsons *like a thematic half- life whose motifs contaminate the multi- layered, intertextual narratives of each episode, often as satire."* (2004: 245)

At this background, Anne Washburn's decision to take *The Simpsons,* of all things, as the one part of popular culture that survives inside the people's memories throughout a nuclear apocalypse, seems even more peculiar and ironic. But that's just what happens in Washburn's "Mr. Burns – A post- electric play". The electric grid is destroyed and people have to adapt to a world without telephones, television, electric stoves or radiators. They have to revert to older ways of engagement, like storytelling, but instead of higher literature they reminisce about parts of popular culture everyone remembers.

The following paper therefore will analyse Anne Washburn's play in regard to the way popular culture is represented in her post- apocalyptic world. Why is it important and why is *The Simpsons* Washburn's main representative of contemporary popular culture in the play? And, moreover, in which ways does the representational form of popular culture change throughout it?

Popular Culture and the play as such

Popular Culture and its importance in modern times

The problem with the term "popular culture" is its vagueness: Contemporary popular culture is almost impossible to define, since it is so widespread. Raymond F. Betts describes this problem in *A History of Popular Culture* this way:

Popular Culture is the first cultural form to compress so many activities previously considered distinct, to engage diverse groups and classes of people so widely in a common environment: in front of the television screen, at the theme park, in the shopping mall, on the computer. [...] The development, still ongoing but less than a century old, has not been premeditated, but it was assured by its two most distinctive characteristics: the proliferation of images and stuff, the intensification of the means of communication and distribution. Add to these two the prevalence of its mood that is entertainment, and the global effects of popular culture are all hunched together. (2013: 157)

At the same time Betts points out that popular culture is mostly uncertain and changeable - no one can certainly determine whether a phenomenon becomes part of popular culture or how long something will stay part of it. (comp. Betts 2013: 157)

While the term popular culture used to refer to the rather vulgar or basic tastes of commoners, its meaning started to change since the 18th century. Popular culture started to denote something `widespread´ (Waltonen/ Du Vernay 2010: **P**2717). The abbreviated form "pop" was coined in England in the late 1950s and was used to entitle art inspired by consumerism and music directed to the youth (Betts 2013: 2). Today, "pop culture envelopes all trends and tastes in a given culture, including film, television, and music." (Waltonen/ Du Vernay 2010: **P**2720). It is, however, not restricted to a culture's consumption habits, but also includes art or various kinds of hobbies, such as dancing, cooking or even knitting.

In 1967, *The Journal of Popular Culture* was founded, which is the official publication of the *Popular Culture Association (*in short: P.C.A.). Both are part of a movement that believes "the perspectives and experiences of common folk offer compelling insights into the social world." (P.C.A. Website: FAQ). The main objective of the journal is to disintegrate the barriers between so- called "low" and "high" culture to create a whole depiction of society by taking into account information popular culture contributes. By no longer neglecting popular culture as a mirror of culture and society, it has "grown more complex and intellectually stimulating in the past thirty years. [...] demanding more cognitive engagement with each passing year." (Johnson quoted in Waltonen/ Du Vernay 2010: **P**2746[1]).

---

1   Please note that in the following the position of quotes in an e-book version of a book will be marked with a "**P**", indicating that it does not refer to a classic page- system.

Already the title of Anne Washburn's play – "Mr. Burns" - shows the importance of the television series *The Simpsons* for her story. But why would the Simpsons, of all things, seem to be a good choice to represent popular culture in a play?

When *The Simpsons* first aired in 1990, its main aim was to polarise the audiences. Matt Groening, the creator of the show, wanted to fabricate a cartoon that would deal with what he called "bigger issues", like love, death or sex, setting his show apart from other cartoon series which only addressed lighter issues. *The Simpsons,* on the other hand, should show topics the audience would really care about (comp. Turner 2005: **P816²**).

Even though the series did not directly top the ratings of long established television series like *The Cosby Show* or *Teenage Mutant Ninja Turtles*, it still registered the third highest income of merchandise products: In 1990 about $750 million were earned by *The Simpsons* products (Turner 2005: **P583**). At this point of the show it was not foreseeable whether *The Simpsons* would survive their next season. Turner describes popular culture as having "the short term memory of a goldfish" (2005: **P625**), thereby indicating how easily one pop culture phenomenon can be replaced by another. Still, about ten years later, *The Simpsons* was watched by an estimate of 60million viewers in circa 70 countries all over the world every week. (Pinsky 2001: 2)

Since its debut, the show's focus does not only rest on its main characters, but incorporates current issues and trends as well as (political) world events. (Turner 2005: **P284**) The characters have to deal with them, thereby introducing topics like religion or politics. (comp. Turner 2005: **P295**). In this way, the show creates a "detailed satirical reflection of the world we live in." (Turner 2005: **P293**)

By using satire as a means of storytelling, *The Simpsons* not always only provokes positive reactions, earning much criticism in the social media, but at the same time evoking higher resonance than most other television series. (Turner 2005: **P594**) This resonance, as Turner points out, is what sets long lasting popular culture phenomena apart from short-lived trends: An audience does not merely consume the series, but connects with it (2005: **P594**). Matt Groening stated in an interview in 2003, that "today's outrage is tomorrow's beloved classic." (in Turner 2005: **P978**). The more attention a topic of the series gets when it first airs, the more likely an audience is to remember it on a longer scale. Turner even tops this comment by claiming that "if there is a common cultural currency, it's got Homer Simpson's picture on it." (2005:**P**284)

It seems that Anne Washburn takes this notion as a starting point for her dystopic play, even stating that if any show could survive an apocalypse, it would be *The Simpsons*, since "so many people enjoy retelling it, mimicking the voices, the gestures; even a terribly reduced population should be able to do a reliable job of putting it back together." (Washburn 2010: IV)

The dystopic setting of Mr. Burns, A post- electric play.

The story of Anne Washburn's *Mr. Burns – A post- electric play* is set in the very near future, as it is stated at the beginning of the play. It starts off with a seemingly normal situation: A group of people sitting together at a campfire, retelling stories of *The Simpsons*. But gradually it becomes clear that this gathering is not a leisure appointment.

The electric grid has disintegrated, leaving the nuclear power plants without electricity to be kept running. As an outcome, the power plants have been destroyed one by one, releasing nuclear radiation that contaminates people and places near to them. Survivors from different cities band together and try to get information about the disposition of people they care about. To do so they keep lists of people they have met along the way, exchanging names with other strangers who have come from different cities.

Since there are no occupations like television or stereo anymore, the people have to return to "the ancient art of storytelling", as Tim Sanford, the artistic director of Playwrights Horizons puts it in the Introduction of the play (Washburn 2010: I). But instead of retelling tales like Shakespeare's *Romeo and Juliet* or the *Iliad* by Homer, they try to retell an episode of *The Simpsons*, which seems to be something most people can remember well.

In the second Act of the play seven years have passed. The main characters seem better adapted to their living situation and they have started to enact *The Simpsons* episodes for audiences in exchange for payment. The emerged theatre field seems to be highly competitive, as other companies earn their living by doing the same as the main characters. The main characters hardly get by and are a very small theatre group in comparison to their competitors. Survivors seem to be desperate and willing to do almost anything to get by. Jenny: "I've gotten people who are hungry, and desperate. I've gotten people who are crazy. [...] Lately people are bold, and that's new." (Washburn 2010: 80f) Additionally, supplies get scarcer. Susannah describes how she has not seen a diet coke in about three years and how such items can be traded for high amounts of goods, like lithium batteries (comp. Washburn 2010: 66ff).

As a result of the people becoming more and more desperate, they start acting corruptly. This becomes clear at the end of the second act, when the main characters get attacked for their goods (comp. Washburn 2010: 96ff). Even though they try to secure themselves with weapons, the scene ends rather abruptly with a blackout. Whether the main characters survive the attack or not is left unclear.

The depiction of Popular Culture in the play

Popular Culture as diversion from reality

At the beginning of "Mr. Burns – A post- electric play", its dystopic setting does not directly come into focus. The main characters are sitting around a fire, retelling an old *The Simpsons* episode while laughing and humming. (comp. Washburn 2010: 2).

Not until the character Gibson enters the scene as a stranger the situation becomes clearer: The characters react with readied weapons, holding him at gun point while searching him for anything dangerous (comp. Washburn 2010: 16f). Throughout their conversation with him, phrases like "How bad is it?" or "Providence was deserted, weirdly, not even a lot of bodies [...]" (Washburn 2010: 18) give a first impression of the dystopic setting of the play. This is further confirmed and specified while the characters talk about what happened and the resulting consequences for them and other people. Especially a story of another survivor told by Susannah expresses the dread the people constantly feel concerning the threats of radiation poisoning and their inability to change the catastrophe coming on (comp. Washburn 2010: 32ff). She describes how the survivor wills his feet not to fail him, ultimately declaring that "it's not knowing [how to stop the nuclear power plants from being destroyed], that's the problem", but not being able to handle the fear. (comp. Washburn 2010:37) This declaration then ultimately leads to a "rather. Long. Pause" (Washburn 2010: 37) in the conversation.

This pause is broken by Gibson, who recites a quote from the *The Simpsons* episode the characters were searching for before. Immediately, all characters jump at the change of subject and start talking about the cartoon series again. At this point, the reminiscence of popular culture phenomena, in this case *The Simpsons* and associated themes like horror movies can be seen as a diversion from the dark reality of the play. The relieved reaction (comp. Washburn 2010: 38) of the character Matt thereby can be interpreted in two different ways: He is either relieved that they finally found the answer to a former question concerning the episode, or he shows his relief because they finally changed the subject to something lighter.

Additionally, it not only seems important to the characters to retell the episode's story in general: They try to remember whole parts of the dialogues, emphasising the importance of exact quotes to keep the comic innuendos of the series. Therefore, in order to be as precise as possible, they rephrase certain quotes and story parts until they reach an acceptable version.

> *Matt: "[...] Oh god wait a minute – uh – uh there's some I remember I remember it's like... there's some,* thing, *where Sideshow Bob keeps meaning to say something dreadful but he says it's some linguistic thing where he says it wrong, "I'm-" - oh, god it's really hard to -"*
>
> *Jenny: "That sounds totally familiar."*
>
> *Matt: "They say something along the lines of, "You can't do this to us," and Sideshow Bob retorts like, "I..." Oh this is torture I know this is really funny...*
>
> *(There is a blankish sort of pause)*
>
> *Matt: "Oh!"*
>
> *Susannah: "Did you get it?"*
>
> *Matt: "No. No, but I just remembered well the whole first act is - [...]."*
>
> *(Washburn 2010:14)*

This need to point out the funny situations in the episode, as opposed to the horror movie background it depicts, can also be seen as a means to escape from reality, using the comic relief of one *The Simpsons* episode as comic relief in a dreary reality.

Furthermore, the retelling of the story is not performed as a mere narration. The characters try to deliver quotes as accurate and lifelike as possible, trying to give the Simpsons characters colour. This can especially be seen in Matt's retelling of the story, for example when he describes Bart's attempt to leave the houseboat:

Matt: [...] and Bart says, (Intake of breath and then) *"Oh no!" and so he runs to the front of the boat and there are piranhas and he says,* (Intake of breath, and then) *"Oh no!" and he runs to the back again and there's all these crocodiles and he's like,* (Intake of breath, and then:) *"Oh... right." (Washburn 2010:43)*

Matt's way of quoting the Simpsons characters makes the other survivors laugh, thereby diverting their attention again from their less happy surroundings. The following performance of musical parts of *Cape Feare* is the character's first step towards theatre acts of *The Simpsons* episodes, which then emerge in the second act of Washburn's play.

Popular Culture as livelihood: Theatre Companies

7 years after the first act, the situation of the play has changed. The survivors are not outside anymore, but inside a "cozy living room" (Washburn 2010:48). At first, it seems as if things have gone back to the normal living standards from before the catastrophe described in the first act: A lamp is glowing in the room, indicating the reinstatement of electricity and when Quincy enters the scene apparently coming from work, she declares she wants to take a "long hot bath" (Washburn 2010: 49). This would either be considered extravagance in a post apocalyptic setting or be impossible because of the lack of electricity, heating and running water.

This positive picture of the characters' situation, however, is destroyed soon after. Colleen declares that she can "see the plug" (Washburn 2010:49), indicating that the whole scene is a fake. It becomes clear that it is an act played at a stage and that the whole situation should resemble life as it was before the disintegration of the electric grid. The lamp light is faked by candles, which seem to be luxury items themselves, as Colleen points out that more of them are "not currently in the budget" (Washburn 2010:50).

The survivors have become a theatre group, performing episodes of *The Simpsons* on stage, rather than just retelling them around a fire as they used to do. The need to bring the episodes to perfection has now gotten a different signification: The closer the re-enactment of an episode gets to the original, the more the audiences, who knew the original episode, will enjoy the performance, therefore increasing the theatre groups' reputation. Gibson and Colleen discuss this later in the act:

> *Gibson: But* Springfield Files *was a great show. People remember loving that episode.*
>
> *Colleen: In the original. Our version sucks. If we don't play it we lose it anyway and every single time we do play it we diminish our reputation.*

Additionally, the group has to deal with business competitions, as different other theatre groups, who also use *The Simpsons* in their performances, exist. Their main competitor is an ensemble called "Richard's" (comp. Washburn 2010:84), which has a bigger team working on it and more props as well as more shows in comparison to the main characters' group. The theatre groups trade shows and props among one another, trying to enhance their own shows. In this way the main characters are negotiating with a theatre group called the "Reruns" to get

8

another *The Simpsons* episode, which they then want to improve with a new line of their own (comp. Washburn 2010: 71f).

Aside from trading whole episodes, the theatre groups also buy lines and stories from outsiders on the street in a so- called booth. This booth, however, entails different issues the main characters have to struggle with. Jenny describes the situation when buying lines as such: "You guys aren't dealing with people. People are making anything up and when I tell them no, thanks, it's starting to get ugly." (Washburn 2010:80) The incapacity of the theatre groups to prove which lines are genuine quotes from a show and which are made up or remembered incorrectly, since there is no way of re-watching the series, leads to a very subjective way of dealing with authenticity. The main characters therefore have to think about securer ways of getting lines, since they cannot compete with other shows that "keep buying lines" (Washburn 2010:81) then.

Even so the other theatre companies have more and possibly better shows, the main characters point out that they have another means of attracting an audience: Quincy: "Our commercials are excellent." (Washburn 2010:85).

Commercials

The re-enactment of commercials in the second act of *Mr. Burns* plays a big role. The homelike scene, which is acted out at the beginning of it, is part of a commercial reminding the audience of products that once were available but are not anymore. Other than advertisements in modern times, the commercials used in the play do not promote one product alone, but provide a whole range of items.

Starting with a voice- over text, like those used in real television advertisements, the audience is addressed directly: "[...] When all you want to say is: Stop the world and let me off [...]. (Washburn 2010:56). This quote instantly expresses the purpose these commercials have: The audience should be removed from the dire surroundings of reality into the dream-like world of the past. Therefore, the use of different well known products in the commercials also adds to the recreation of this past life. Not only familiar brands like "Fanta" or "diet coke" (Washburn 2010: 62) are mentioned, but whole establishments like the French "Prêt a Manger" (Washburn 2010:60) and their famous little sandwiches are brought up.

The reason, why exactly those kinds of products are used in their commercials is given when Gibson scrutinises the use of the wine "Chablis" (Washburn 2010:63) in it: "The point of a commercial is to create a reality which is *welcoming*, not challenging." (Washburn

9

2010:64). Thus, the group tries to use products which are either well- remembered or liked because of other reasons like "the pure sound pleasure" or the feelings a certain item conveys (Washburn 2010:63) .

Another way of creating a feeling of reminiscence is the use of smell. Jenny wants to incorporate bath salt smell into the commercial, thereby triggering memories of real baths of the past in the audience (comp. Washburn 2010:65). The problem arising with that is the subjectivity: If a person did not like that smell before, it will rather disturb his or her reception of the commercial than enhance it.

While the others try to create a welcoming and cosy feeling in the audience, Gibson wants to change the commercials according to the way they were before the catastrophe. He indicates how advertising was used to exploit people and how there was a "question of identity. Like it's not just what is desire, it's who has the desire." (Washburn 2010: 64). This notion is then blocked by the other main characters, who believe it to be a joke.

Music and Popular Culture

The use of music has different effects in the play. In the first act music can be seen as part of the survivor's memories. The *The Simpsons* episode "Cape Feare" is a parody of different well known Horror Movies, referencing amongst others *A nightmare on Elm Street* (1984), Alfred Hitchcock's *Psycho* (1960) and obviously both movie versions of *Cape Fear* (1962/1991), which the title points out. In films, musical scores are often associated with certain narrative contents. Patrick N. Juslin and Daniel Västfjäll take up the example of Steven Spielberg's *Jaws*, in which two repeated musical notes represent the proximity of the villain, namely the great white shark (comp. 2008: 578). This concept is also applicable to *Cape Fear*'s main musical score, which basically consists of a repeating sound pattern of dark tunes. The main score in this horror movie is used to foreshadow the narrative content, creating a haunting and uncanny atmosphere. At the same time it amplifies the narrative content in important scenes, for example when the villain appears onscreen for the first time.

In the *The Simpsons* episode "Cape Feare", the musical score from the original movie is used, but reduced to its first repeating tunes. These might be the most memorable part of the score since the main characters in Anne Washburn's *Mr. Burns* remember them quite well. Matt: "[...] and it's like whomp whomp – well yeah that's the sound from the Cape Fear soundtrack that's the – whomp whomp whomp" (Washburn 2010: 2), at which point the other characters join in a chorus. Therefore, at this point, the music not only exists as part of the cartoon episode the characters want to retell, but at the same time makes them remember other parts of popular culture, scilicet the genre of horror movies.

Another musical reference in the first act is the scores by Gilbert and Sullivan. While the characters at first only try to remember the lyrics which were sung in the cartoon episode and the way in which they were performed, they soon realize one of them, Gibson, is able to recite the whole music, since he was part of a "small amateur society" (Washburn 2010: 45). The characters then request him to sing "The three little maids from school are we" from *The Mikado*, urging him on, even though Washburn emphasises in a side note that the characters are not the kind of people who, "in their previous life, would have enjoyed the idea of an impromptu Gilbert & Sullivan recital" (2010: 45). Even so, some time later Gibson teaches the other characters a song, which they seem to enjoy as they "stumble and giggle through it" (Washburn 2010: 47). The musical performance of this song forms the end of the first act, thereby showing in which way the characters' lives have changed. Music, which had had a mere background function, now becomes part of their engagement, giving them something to do without electricity.

In the second Act the dystopic world has changed. It is seven years later and the group of survivors have become a theatrical group that re-enacts episodes from *The Simpsons*. Music, in this context, is not only used for *The Simpsons* theme, but also in commercials the group performs. In commercials, the role of music is very important:

"[...] when [background music is] used appropriately, [it] is the catalyst of advertising. It augments pictures and colors words, and often adds a form of energy available through no other source." (Hecker 1984: 442)

While in today's time this quote refers to the ability of music to make a commercial more appealing to possible customers, the music's benefit in the play is a different one. The characters want to create a new reality, in which the audience is reminded of better times (comp. Washburn 2010: 54ff). Music is a so-called sensory stimuli, that can trigger memories of past emotional events. These memories then can re-create these past emotions in a person. (Gökçay; Gülsen 2010: 353) In this way the structure of a musical piece or its bond to a memory can affect the audience's emotional experience.

Another part of the group's show is a medley of "popular hits from the last 10 years" (Washburn 2010: 88). This again shows a way in which popular culture is depicted throughout the play. Not only one, but different well known songs are used, illustrating the vast variety of electronic media the people were used to. The utilised lyrics as such seem like

11

a mirror of the characters' situation: Sentences like "It's the end of everything we are." or "I'm drenched with my tears" (Washburn 2010: 89) reflect the dystopic setting in which the characters had to deal with new living situations and start their lives over on completely different premises.

The last act, which is set 75 years later, is then a complete musical. It is the performance of a *The Simpsons* episode which is completely choreographed, retelling the story of a catastrophe. The first thing that is striking about the music in this act is the change of music genres: While the musical starts out with the "Chorus of the Shades of Springfield" (Washburn 2010: 100), which is disrupted by individual characters singing on their own before rejoining the group, distinctive characters also set a change in the music's rhythm, for example Nelson with a "half rap" (Washburn 2010: 101). This can be interpreted as a character trait of Nelson that survived the years, depicting his rebellious and youthful side. It is part of his characterisation as troublemaker in the original series and can be seen as a small part of popular culture that survived the apocalypse.

When the part of the play- inside- the- play begins that resembles the episode *Cape Feare*, the opening score of *The Simpsons* is sung, but it is different from the original. "They sing a slightly eerie and way more complex variant of the Simpson's theme song" (Washburn 2010:106), which is intermingled with thunder. Again, this choice of music underlines the dark setting of both plays – Washburn's dystopic future scenario and the play acted out inside it. The jolly and fleeting theme song of the cartoon series now depicts the dangerous and deathly environment of the story, thereby already foreshadowing the loss of comic relief in the *The Simpsons* episode which is acted out.

While a medley of popular music was performed in the second act, bits and pieces of those songs can be found in the third act, as well. They are partly changed to fit into the character's speech parts but still recognisable. In this way, for example, Britney Spears' popular song *Toxic* can be discovered in the play, even though it has been denoted as being "a piece of music which does not play well with others" in the preceding act. The original lyrics,

With the taste of your lips I'm on a ride. You're toxic, I'm slipping under. With the taste of the poison paradise I'm addicted to you. Don't you know that you're toxic? (Spears 2004: Booklet)

are changed to fit into Mr. Burn's dialogue, depicting himself as being toxic:

With one touch to your lips It's homicide (He's toxic you're slipping under) Just one taste of my poison paradise. You're afflicted by me yes you know that I'm toxic. (Washburn 2010: 118f)

The use of *Toxic* as part of Mr. Burns' dialogue supports the statement from the second act: Just as the song does not get along with other songs, Mr. Burns is a character who apparently does not get along with other characters, either.

This is an example how contemporary popular culture is taken and changed in the play to fit the circumstances, while at the same time still showing the high influence a song as part of popular culture can have. In Washburn's dystopic setting the song is being remembered more than 80 years after its release, even though original recordings are not available.

Moreover, the medley performed in the second act is taken up during the final act when a song "recalls the high point of [it]" (Washburn 2010: 120). In this way ties are established between the topics of the play- inside- the- play and the situation of the survivors in the first two acts, hinting at a change in regards of content of the performed episode. It is not only a re-enactment of *The Simpsons' Cape Feare*, but has changed its story according to the play's own history.

Popular Culture merged with reality

The third act of Washburn's play takes place in a changed world compared to that of the second act. 75 years have passed and all the audience sees is a play: The actors are in costumes, which "bear a blurred similarity to faces we may recall from the tv series" (Washburn 2010: 100) and the words are sung instead of recited.

At the beginning, well known characters from *The Simpsons*, like Ned Flanders or Nelson, start telling the situation. They describe a blaring siren and a call over the radio (comp. Washburn 2010: 100f). But instead of evacuating the city, the characters move towards the part of town "where flames leapt in the air" (Washburn 2010:101). It becomes clear that the Nuclear Power plant of the fictional town Springfield caught fire and exploded and the characters repeatedly emphasise how "no one thought to flee" (comp. Washburn 2010: 102ff). At this point, the similarities between the main characters' fate in the first act and the destiny of the residents of Springfield can easily be spotted. The characters portray how death in form of radiation slowly kills the people who do not flee fast enough: "The wind is filled with hunger – Our bodies are a feast." (Washburn 2010: 104). Survivors try to get away, but only one family "runs from their history, runs toward their destiny" (Washburn 2010: 105) – The Simpsons.

From this point on, the play- inside- the- play resembles the *The Simpsons* episode "Cape Feare", which the survivors try to put together in the first act. As in the first act version, the Simpson family resides on a houseboat, fleeing from their old life (Washburn 2010:106). But while the family tried to get away from one villain, Sideshow Bob, in the original episode, this time they are running from a catastrophe. Again, similarities between the dystopic reality depicted in Washburn's play and the situation in this play- inside- the-play can be seen. Marge and Lisa mention the lack of electricity and light (comp. Washburn 2010: 108) and they express the wish to see everything they had to leave behind again (Washburn 2010:109). Also the detachment from former rules is brought up, but Bart and Homer do not seem to share the sentimental feelings of the female family members (Washburn 2010: 109).

When the whole family decides to go below, a villain appears on the boat, just as it happens in the original episode. But it is not Sideshow Bob who appears onstage: Mr. Burns, the "ancient billionaire tyrant" (Turner 2005: P10605) and owner of the Springfield nuclear power plant climbs onto the houseboat. At first, the appearance of Mr. Burns as main villain instead of Sideshow Bob can be seen as an adjustment to the new theme of the story: The Simpsons are fleeing the catastrophe and Mr. Burns, as the power plant's owner and Homer's former boss, is the figurative trigger of it. At the time it becomes clear that this manifestation of Mr. Burns is more than just a normal human being: Whatever he touches literally burns. (comp. Washburn 2010:113) "There is the sound of sizzling flesh. Homer sinks, dead, to the ground." (Washburn 2010:118). In this way, Mr. Burns can not only be seen as the trigger of the catastrophe, but as the poisonous effect of it itself. He is the deathly radioactivity following the Simpson family during their escape.

While, during the first act of Washburn's play, *The Simpsons* was used as a means to escape the dreadful reality and to reminisce about better times, reality and fiction have merged in the last act. The characters no longer try to re-enact original episodes, but seem to process their own fate in the story. The villain is changed from just any *The Simpsons* villain to the one person connected to what is called "nuclearism" in psychopathology (comp. Broderick 2004: 246) – Mr. Burns- thereby showing a need of the people to find a somehow concrete villain to blame for their fate. Additionally, the whole atmosphere of the episode is changed. The original episode, though dealing with the attempted murder of Bart, is filled with moments of comic relief, for example when Bart and Sideshow Bob duet together. In the play- inside- the- play, even though parts of the original dialogue are adopted into the act, the

14

comic relief of the same lines changes into a darker, graver meaning: *Bart: "This is it Burns. You're never coming back." Burns: (sly, mocking) "What, never?" Bart: "No, never!"*(Washburn 2010: 129f).

At the end of Anne Washburn's play the survivor's feelings on their situation becomes clear: While in the original *The Simpsons* episode the whole Simpson family survives Sideshow Bob's attack, in the play- inside- the- play the ending is different. Mr. Burns kills everybody except for Bart, who in the end defeats the evil villain. The chorus depicts the breaking dawn in a positive way: The clouds have parted, the rainfall has stopped, there are chittering birds and "the warm wind of the morning" (comp. Washburn 2010: 130). Still, Bart notes how he "lost everything" and that everyone he loved is gone forever (Washburn 2010: 131), thereby reflecting the fate of the survivors in the first act, who did not know what happened to their loved ones.

As the character of Mr. Burns pointed out before, "this is no Victory Bart Simpson" (Washburn 2010:129), since he is the lone survivor. Still, the climax of the third act ends with a group song, sung "to the tune of Gilbert and Sullivan's *For He Is An Englishman*" (Washburn 2010: 132). The song depicts the American fate, suddenly stressing that *The Simpsons* are an ordinary American family. The message conveyed by the song is one of continuity and a better future, thereby indirectly indicating the notion of the American dream:

But though swept from our foundations

 Through our steely endurations

 (O we remain American

 For we remain Ameriiiicaaaaaan!)   *(Washburn 2010:132)*

The end of the play, especially the sudden use of uniting term "American", again shows how the reality of the play and that of the popular culture phenomenon seem to have merged together. *The Simpsons* are used as representatives for all people who suffered the dystopic fate and thereby changed from a simple popular culture phenomenon to a means of dealing with reality.

Conclusion

In a nutshell, contemporary popular culture is an ever- changing field, which is never finished and can change in a heartbeat. Still, those phenomena which stay part of popular culture for some time will take up a part of the memory of the people, thereby carving society and culture.

The Simpsons, as a series which has been part of popular culture for more than 20 years now, reflects our culture in a challenging way, trying to make society think about itself. It therefore provides the basis to survive an apocalypse in the minds and hearts of its audience, which Homer Simpson started capturing in the 1990s, as Chris Turner puts it. (2005: **P2420**)

In Anne Washburn's *Mr. Burns, A Post- Electric Play,* popular culture is used for different purposes. It starts out as a pastime for the survivors of a catastrophe who do not have other amusements any longer. At the same time, popular culture supplies the people with a shelter from their harsh reality, keeping the memories of better times alive in their heads.

It then changes and becomes not only a kind of currency, as people can trade in quotes and episodes from television series, but also helps to form a new theatre community, which then evolves into a way of staying alive in a changed world.

At last, popular culture even becomes part of the reality. The people use popular culture to narrate their own history, by this way coming to terms with their own fate. By highlighting the positive future that lies ahead in comparison to the past, popular culture creates a basis for the people to carry on with their lives in a more positive way.

References

Primary Literature:

Washburn, Anne. 2010. *Mr. Burns, A post- Electric Play*. New York: Smith & Kraus.

Secondary Literature:

Betts, Raymond F. & Bly, Lyz. 2013 [2004]. *A History of Popular Culture: More of Everything, Faster and Brighter*. Second Edition. New York: Routledge.

Broderick, Mick. 2004. *Releasing the Hounds: The Simpsons As Anti- Nuclear Satire.* in: Alberti, John. *Leaving Springfield –* The Simpsons *and the Possibility of Oppositional Culture.* Detroit: Wayne State University Press

Gökçay, Didem; Gülsen, Yildrim. 2010. *Affective Computing and Interaction: Psychological, Cognitive and Neuroscientific Perspectives*. New York: IGI Global

Hecker, Sidney. 1984. *Music for Advertising Effect.* Psychology & Marketing Volume 4. In: Allen, David. 2006. *Effects of Popular Music in Advertising on Attention and Memory.* Journal of Advertising Research Volume 46. p. 343-444.

Juslin, Patrick N.; Västfjäl, Daniel. 2008. *Emotional responses to music: The need to consider underlying mechanisms.* in: Behavioral & Brain Sciences. 31.5: 559-621.

Pinsky, Mark. 2001. *The Gospel According to the Simpsons.* Luisville: Westminster John Knox Press.

Turner, Chris. 2004. *Planet Simpson: How a Cartoon Masterpiece Documented an Era and Defined a Generation.* ebook- Version. London: Ebury Press.

Waltonen, Karma; Du Vernay, Denise. 2010. *The Simpsons in the Classroom.* ebook-Version. North Carolina: Mc Farland & Company.

Internet Sources & Others:

Popular Culture Association (P.C.A.). *The Journal of Popular Culture.* Information Site. Dec. 10, 2014. http://www.journalofpopularculture.com

Spears, Britney. 2004. *Greatest Hits: My Prerogative.* Music Album Booklet. New York: Jive Records.